# SRA Reading Mastery

CLASSIC EDITION

# Behavioral Objectives

# Level I

**Siegfried Engelmann**
**Elaine C. Bruner**

*A Division of The* **McGraw·Hill** *Companies*

*Columbus, Ohio*

**www.sra4kids.com**

*SRA/McGraw-Hill*

*A Division of The McGraw·Hill Companies*

# INTRODUCTION

The *Reading Mastery* programs are based on the underlying concept that all children can learn if carefully taught. The programs provide the kind of careful instruction that is needed to teach basic reading skills.

The sequence of skills in *Reading Mastery* Classic Edition, Level I is controlled so that the student is able to perform confidently the skills at each step before going on to more complicated tasks. Teacher-directed activities include lessons on prereading, sound-letter relationships, decoding, reading vocabulary, oral reading, and comprehension. In the area of reading and picture comprehension, independent written activities relate to the stories that students are reading. Worksheet exercises offer practice in sound writing, pattern recognition, matching, and picture completion.

In the spelling part of the program, the student writes sounds, words, and sentences that the teacher dictates. Spelling words follow the sequence of reading words taught in the program.

## Scope and Sequence Chart
The Scope and Sequence chart on page 3 provides a quick overview of *Reading Mastery I*. The chart lists the various tracks (skills) that are taught and the range of lessons for each track.

## Behavioral Objectives
This booklet gives a comprehensive picture of *Reading Mastery I*. It focuses on the general curriculum goals of the program and on special behavioral goals to be achieved by individual students.

The Behavioral Objectives, which begin on page 4, cover the major skill areas, or tracks, shown on the Scope and Sequence chart. Above each chart is the name of the track and the range of lessons in which it appears. The chart itself is divided into four sections:

• The **Purpose of the track** is the general curriculum objective.

• The **Behavioral objective** is the kind of performance that can be expected from the student who has mastered the skill.

• The section headed **The student is asked to** describes the specific kinds of tasks the student performs in order to master the skill.

• The section headed **First appears in** shows where the skill is first introduced in the program.

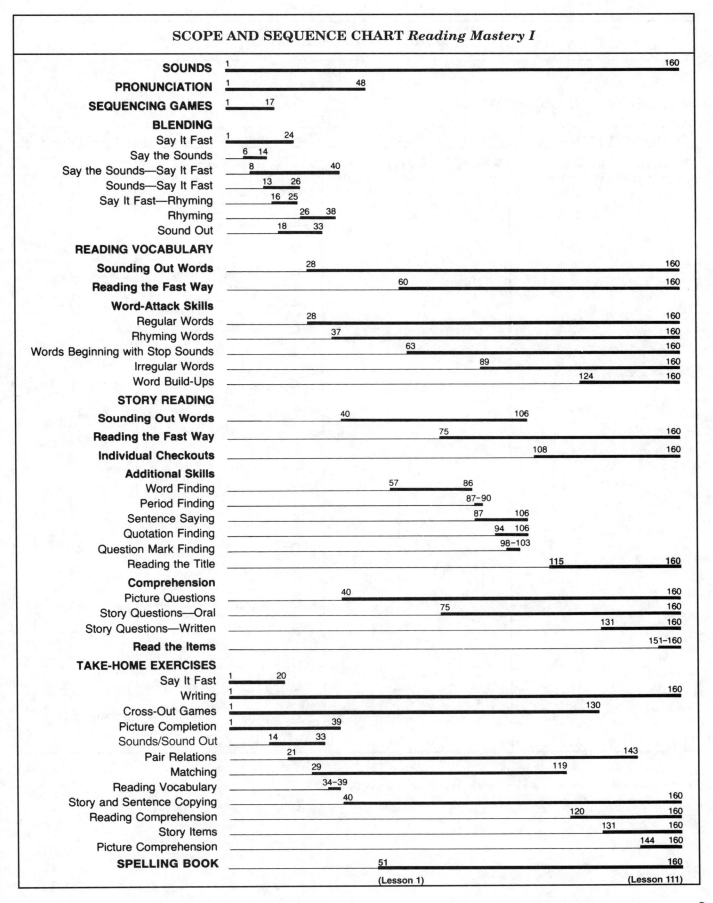

# SCOPE AND SEQUENCE CHART *Reading Mastery I*

| | |
|---|---|
| **SOUNDS** | 1 —— 160 |
| **PRONUNCIATION** | 1 —— 48 |
| **SEQUENCING GAMES** | 1 — 17 |
| **BLENDING** | |
| Say It Fast | 1 —— 24 |
| Say the Sounds | 6 — 14 |
| Say the Sounds—Say It Fast | 8 —— 40 |
| Sounds—Say It Fast | 13 — 26 |
| Say It Fast—Rhyming | 16 — 25 |
| Rhyming | 26 — 38 |
| Sound Out | 18 — 33 |
| **READING VOCABULARY** | |
| **Sounding Out Words** | 28 —— 160 |
| **Reading the Fast Way** | 60 —— 160 |
| **Word-Attack Skills** | |
| Regular Words | 28 —— 160 |
| Rhyming Words | 37 —— 160 |
| Words Beginning with Stop Sounds | 63 —— 160 |
| Irregular Words | 89 —— 160 |
| Word Build-Ups | 124 —— 160 |
| **STORY READING** | |
| **Sounding Out Words** | 40 —— 106 |
| **Reading the Fast Way** | 75 —— 160 |
| **Individual Checkouts** | 108 —— 160 |
| **Additional Skills** | |
| Word Finding | 57 —— 86 |
| Period Finding | 87–90 |
| Sentence Saying | 87 —— 106 |
| Quotation Finding | 94 — 106 |
| Question Mark Finding | 98–103 |
| Reading the Title | 115 —— 160 |
| **Comprehension** | |
| Picture Questions | 40 —— 160 |
| Story Questions—Oral | 75 —— 160 |
| Story Questions—Written | 131 —— 160 |
| **Read the Items** | 151–160 |
| **TAKE-HOME EXERCISES** | |
| Say It Fast | 1 — 20 |
| Writing | 1 —— 160 |
| Cross-Out Games | 1 —— 130 |
| Picture Completion | 1 — 39 |
| Sounds/Sound Out | 14 — 33 |
| Pair Relations | 21 —— 143 |
| Matching | 29 —— 119 |
| Reading Vocabulary | 34–39 |
| Story and Sentence Copying | 40 —— 160 |
| Reading Comprehension | 120 —— 160 |
| Story Items | 131 —— 160 |
| Picture Comprehension | 144 — 160 |
| **SPELLING BOOK** | 51 —— 160 |
| | (Lesson 1)      (Lesson 111) |

## SOUNDS: SOUND RECOGNITION

Range of Lessons: 1-160

| Purpose of the track | Behavioral objectives | The student is asked to | First appears in |
|---|---|---|---|
| To teach the student the sounds associated with letters (printed symbols) | When given a printed symbol, the student is able to recognize and produce the sound represented by the symbol. | Say the sounds represented by the following symbols: | |

The student is asked to:

Say the sounds represented by the following symbols:

| Symbol | Sound | As in | First appears in |
|---|---|---|---|
| **a** | aaa | <u>a</u>nd | Lesson 1 (12)* |
| **m** | mmm | ra<u>m</u> | Lesson 4 (11) |
| **s** | sss | bu<u>s</u> | Lesson 9 (16) |
| **ē** | ēēē | <u>ea</u>t | Lesson 19 |
| **r** | rrr | ba<u>r</u> | Lesson 23 |
| **d** | d | ma<u>d</u> | Lesson 27 |
| **f** | fff | stu<u>ff</u> | Lesson 31 |
| **i** | iii | <u>i</u>f | Lesson 34 |
| **th** | ththth | <u>th</u>is (not thing) | Lesson 38 |
| **ī** | t | ca<u>t</u> | Lesson 41 |
| **n** | nnn | pa<u>n</u> | Lesson 44 |
| **c** | c | ta<u>ck</u> | Lesson 48 |
| **o** | ooo | <u>o</u>x | Lesson 51 |
| **ā** | āāā | <u>a</u>te | Lesson 58 |
| **h** | h | <u>h</u>at | Lesson 61 |
| **u** | uuu | <u>u</u>nder | Lesson 64 |
| **g** | g | ta<u>g</u> | Lesson 68 |

(continued)

*Numbers in parentheses are for students who enter the program at Lesson 11.

| Purpose of the track | Behavioral objectives | The student is asked to | First appears in |
|---|---|---|---|
| | | Say the sounds represented by the following symbols: | |

| Symbol | Sound | As in | First appears in |
|---|---|---|---|
| l | lll | pa_l_ | Lesson 72 |
| w | www | wo_w_ | Lesson 76 |
| sh | shshsh | wi_sh_ | Lesson 80 |
| I | (the word I) | | Lesson 88 |
| k | k | tac_k_ | Lesson 92 |
| ō | ōōō | _o_ver | Lesson 98 |
| v | vvv | lo_v_e | Lesson 102 |
| p | p | sa_p_ | Lesson 108 |
| ch | ch | tou_ch_ | Lesson 113 |
| e | eee | _e_nd | Lesson 118 |
| b | b | gra_b_ | Lesson 121 |
| ing | iiing | s_ing_ | Lesson 124 |
| ī | īīī | _i_ce | Lesson 127 |
| y | yyy | _y_ard | Lesson 131 |
| er | urrr/errr | broth_er_ | Lesson 135 |
| x | ksss | o_x_ | Lesson 139 |
| oo | oooo | m_oo_n (not look) | Lesson 142 |
| j | j | ju_dg_e | Lesson 145 |
| ȳ | ȳȳȳ/īīī | m_y_ | Lesson 149 |
| wh | www or wh | _wh_y | Lesson 152 |
| qu | kwww/koo | _qu_ick | Lesson 154 |
| z | zzz | bu_zz_ | Lesson 156 |
| ū | ūūū | _u_se | Lesson 158 |

| Purpose of the track | Behavioral objectives | The student is asked to | First appears in |
|---|---|---|---|
| To provide practice in pronouncing sounds | When given a sound orally, the student is able to pronounce the sound. | Pronounce a sound after it has been presented orally | |
| | | mmm | Lesson 1 (11)* |
| | | ăăă | Lesson 1 (11) |
| | | d | Lesson 2 (14) |
| | | ēēē | Lesson 3 (19) |
| | | fff | Lesson 3 (11) |
| | | rrr | Lesson 4 (13) |
| | | sss | Lesson 4 (13) |
| | | ththth | Lesson 5 (12) |
| | | zzz | Lesson 6 |
| | | ĭĭĭ | Lesson 9 (12) |
| | | ŏŏŏ | Lesson 14 |
| | | t | Lesson 15 |
| | | ōōō | Lesson 16 |
| | | nnn | Lesson 19 |
| | | c | Lesson 34 |
| | | āāā | Lesson 41 |
| | | vvv | Lesson 48 |
| | | ŭŭŭ | Lesson 48 |

*Numbers in parentheses are for students who enter the program at Lesson 11.

## SEQUENCING GAMES

Range of Lessons: 1-17

| Purpose of the track | Behavioral objectives | The student is asked to | First appears in |
|---|---|---|---|
| To teach the student to sequence events in order | When shown an action sequence pictured on an arrow, the student is able to perform the pictured actions in order. | Perform a pictured sequence of actions, following an arrow from left to right | Lesson 1 (11)* |
| | When given the direction "first" or "next" for an action sequence, the student is able to respond with the appropriate action. | Perform the "first" and "next" actions pictured on an arrow; then perform the actions without looking at the pictures | Lesson 13 |

## BLENDING: SAY IT FAST

Range of Lessons: 1-24

| Purpose of the track | Behavioral objectives | The student is asked to | First appears in |
|---|---|---|---|
| To help the student understand the relationship between the sounds in a word and the word that is formed | When the teacher says a word slowly, the student is able to say the word at a normal rate. | Say at a normal rate a compound or multisyllable word that the teacher has presented slowly *with a pause* between two parts | Lesson 1 |
| | | Say at a normal rate a word that the teacher has presented slowly with the sounds lengthened and *no pause* between the sounds | Lesson 4 (11)* |

## BLENDING: SAY THE SOUNDS

Range of Lessons: 6-14

| Purpose of the track | Behavioral objectives | The student is asked to | First appears in |
|---|---|---|---|
| To teach the student that words are composed of blended sounds | The student is able to say a word slowly, one sound at a time, without pausing between the sounds. | Say the sounds in a word that consists of two or three continuous sounds | Lesson 6 (11)* |
| | | Say the sounds in a two- or three-sound word that ends in a stop sound | Lesson 9 (11) |

*Numbers in parentheses are for students who enter the program at Lesson 11.

## BLENDING: SAY THE SOUNDS—SAY IT FAST

**Range of Lessons: 8-40**

| Purpose of the track | Behavioral objectives | The student is asked to | First appears in |
|---|---|---|---|
| To consolidate the skills of saying words slowly and saying words fast | When the teacher says a word slowly, the student is able to repeat the word slowly and then say it fast. | Say a word slowly; then say it fast | Lesson 8 (11)* |

## BLENDING: SOUNDS—SAY IT FAST

**Range of Lessons: 13-26**

| Purpose of the track | Behavioral objectives | The student is asked to | First appears in |
|---|---|---|---|
| To teach the student the blending skills of saying a single written sound slowly and then saying it fast | When presented with a single or repeated symbol of a sound, the student is able to say the sound slowly and then say it fast. | Say a written sound slowly; then say it fast | Lesson 13 |

## BLENDING: SAY IT FAST—RHYMING

**Range of Lessons: 16-25**

| Purpose of the track | Behavioral objectives | The student is asked to | First appears in |
|---|---|---|---|
| To teach the student to blend words that have two parts—an initial sound followed by an ending | When the teacher orally presents a word that has two parts—a beginning sound and an ending—the student is able to say the word parts slowly and then say the word fast. | Say a two-part word slowly; then say it fast | Lesson 16 |

*Number in parentheses is for students who enter the program at Lesson 11.

## BLENDING: RHYMING

Range of Lessons: 26-38

| Purpose of the track | Behavioral objectives | The student is asked to | First appears in |
|---|---|---|---|
| To teach the student to rhyme | When the teacher orally presents a word ending, the student is able to produce a rhyming word by blending a specified initial sound with the ending. | Blend a sound with an ending to make a rhyming word | Lesson 26 |

## BLENDING: SOUND OUT

Range of Lessons: 18-33

| Purpose of the track | Behavioral objectives | The student is asked to | First appears in |
|---|---|---|---|
| To teach the student to blend written sounds | When presented with two sounds written on an arrow, the student is able to say the sounds from left to right, slowly blending the sounds without pausing. | Say the sounds on an arrow slowly without stopping between sounds | Lesson 18 |
| | | Touch under and say the sounds on an arrow slowly without stopping between sounds | Take-Home 19 |

## READING VOCABULARY: REGULAR WORDS

Range of Lessons: 28-160

| Purpose of the track | Behavioral objectives | The student is asked to | First appears in |
|---|---|---|---|
| To teach the student to decode regular words | The student is able first to sound out a regular word that begins with a continuous sound and then say the word at a normal rate. | Sound out and say a two- or three-sound word | Lesson 28 |
| | The student is able to read some familiar words without sounding them out first. | Read *some* words "the fast way" without sounding out first | Lesson 65 |
| | The student is able to read most words, new and old, without sounding out first. | Read *most* words "the fast way" without sounding out first | Lesson 96 |

## READING VOCABULARY: RHYMING WORDS

**Range of Lessons: 37-160**

| Purpose of the track | Behavioral objectives | The student is asked to | First appears in |
|---|---|---|---|
| To teach the student to recognize and read word families by using rhyming skills | When given two or more rhyming words, the student is able to read the words by blending each initial sound with the ending. | Read two or more words by blending different initial sounds with the same ending | Lesson 37 |

## READING VOCABULARY: WORDS BEGINNING WITH STOP SOUNDS

**Range of Lessons: 63-160**

| Purpose of the track | Behavioral objectives | The student is asked to | First appears in |
|---|---|---|---|
| To teach the student to decode words that begin with stop sounds | When given a word that begins with a stop sound, the student is able to use rhyming skills to decode the word. | Read a word that begins with a stop sound by first sounding out the rhyming element and then adding the initial sound | Lesson 63 |

## READING VOCABULARY: IRREGULAR WORDS

**Range of Lessons: 89-160**

| Purpose of the track | Behavioral objectives | The student is asked to | First appears in |
|---|---|---|---|
| To teach the student to discriminate between the way an irregular word is sounded out and the way it is said | When given an irregular word, the student is able to sound out the word and then say it as it is usually said. | Sound out an irregular word and then say the word | Lesson 89 |
| | | Read an irregular word the fast way; then alternate sounding out and saying the word | Lesson 92 |

| Purpose of the track | Behavioral objectives | The student is asked to | First appears in |
|---|---|---|---|
| To teach the student to decode words with endings such as *ed, ing, er,* and *s* and words that begin with two consonants | *Endings:* When given a word with an ending, the student is able to identify the word, identify the ending, and then read the whole word. | Read words with the following endings: | |
| | | ed | Lesson 124 |
| | | ing | Lesson 132 |
| | | er | Lesson 143 |
| | | s | Lesson 154 |
| | *Initial consonant blends:* When given a word that begins with two consonants, the student is able first to blend the beginning sound with the rest of the word; then to sound out the whole word; and finally to say the whole word fast. | Read words beginning with the following consonant blends: | |
| | | sl | Lesson 125 |
| | | st | Lesson 129 |
| | | br | Lesson 137 |
| | | sw | Lesson 148 |
| | | fl | Lesson 152 |
| | | sm | Lesson 155 |
| | | tr | Lesson 156 |
| | | cr | Lesson 160 |

## STORY READING: SOUNDING OUT WORDS

**Range of Lessons: 40-106**

| Purpose of the track | Behavioral objectives | The student is asked to | First appears in |
|---|---|---|---|
| To teach the student to apply to story reading the skills learned in reading vocabulary exercises | When given a story, the student is able to sound out and then say fast each word in the story. | Sound out and then say fast the words in the following kinds of stories: | |
| | | 2-word stories | Lesson 40 |
| | | 1-sentence stories | Lesson 48 |
| | | 2-sentence stories | Lesson 70 |
| | | 3- to 7-sentence stories | Lesson 80 |
| | | 2-page stories | Lesson 99 |

## STORY READING: READING THE FAST WAY

**Range of Lessons: 75-160**

| Purpose of the track | Behavioral objectives | The student is asked to | First appears in |
|---|---|---|---|
| To teach the student to read a story accurately at a normal rate | When asked to read a story, the student is able to read the words at a normal rate, sounding out unknown words only. | Sound out the story; then reread the first sentence the fast way | Lesson 75 |
| | | Sound out the story; then reread the first two sentences the fast way | Lesson 87 |
| | | Sound out the story; then reread the entire story the fast way | Lesson 91 |
| | | Read the entire story the fast way on the first reading | Lesson 107 |

| Purpose of the track | Behavioral objectives | The student is asked to | | | | Appears in |
|---|---|---|---|---|---|---|
| To teach the student to read with increased speed and accuracy | The student reads a previously-read selection in a specified period of time with an error limit. | Read out loud at the following rates without exceeding the error limits: | | | | |
| | | Error limit | Number of words read | No. of minutes | Words per minute | |
| | | 3 | 41 | 2.5 | 16 | Lesson 108 |
| | | 3 | 35 | 2.0 | 18 | Lesson 109 |
| | | 3 | 43 | 2.0 | 22 | Lesson 110 |
| | | 3 | 49 | 2.0 | 25 | Lesson 115 |
| | | 3 | 44 | 2.0 | 22 | Lesson 120 |
| | | 3 | 89 | 3.0 | 30 | Lesson 125 |
| | | 3 | 107 | 3.0 | 36 | Lesson 130 |
| | | 3 | 112 | 3.0 | 37 | Lesson 135 |
| | | 3 | 92 | 2.5 | 37 | Lesson 140 |
| | | 3 | 107 | 3.0 | 36 | Lesson 145 |
| | | 4 | 133 | 3.5 | 38 | Lesson 150 |
| | | 3 | 100 | 2.5 | 40 | Lesson 155 |
| | | 3 | 95 | 2.5 | 38 | Lesson 160 |

| Purpose of the track | Behavioral objectives | The student is asked to | Range of lessons |
|---|---|---|---|
| Word finding<br>To give the student practice in finding a word after hearing it pronounced | When the teacher tells what word to look for, the student is able to identify the correct word. | Touch a word that has been previously sounded out | Lessons 57 – 86 |
| Period finding<br>To teach the student how to find the end of a sentence | When shown the beginning of a sentence, the student is able to find the period that ends the sentence. | Move along an arrow, touching each word until reaching the period at the end of the sentence | Lessons 87 – 90 |
| Sentence saying<br>To teach the student to repeat a whole sentence | After reading a sentence word by word, the student is able to repeat the sentence from memory at a normal speaking rate with an inflection that conveys meaning. | Say from memory a whole sentence previously read word by word | Lessons 87 – 106 |
| Quotation finding<br>To teach the student that quotation marks designate spoken words | When given a quotation, the student is able to recognize that the quotation marks designate spoken words and to say the quotation. | Touch the quotation marks in a story<br><br>Read and repeat the quotation | Lessons 94 – 106 |
| Question mark finding<br>To teach the student the difference between a question and a statement | When given a written question, the student is able to recognize that the sentence asks a question. | Touch a question mark at the end of a sentence<br><br>Read the question and repeat it at a normal speaking rate | Lessons 98 – 103 |
| Reading the title<br>To teach the student to identify the title of a story | When given the title of a story, the student is able to tell what the story is about. | Tell what a story is about from its title | Lessons 115 – 160 |

| Purpose of the track | Behavioral objectives | The student is asked to | First appears in |
|---|---|---|---|
| Picture questions<br>To teach the student the relationship between a story and a picture | *Predictions:* After reading a story, the student is able to predict what will be seen in a related picture. | Answer questions or complete items to tell what will be in a picture | Lesson 40 |
| | *Questions:* When given a picture that goes with a story, the student is able to answer questions directly related to the picture. | Answer factual questions requiring judgments about the story | Lesson 40 |
| | *Story Illustration:* After reading a sentence related to the story, the student is able to draw a picture based on the story sentence. | Draw a picture that shows the story sentence. | Take-Home 91<br>Plain paper 120 |
| Story questions—oral<br>To teach the student to focus on the meaning of a story while reading | When rereading a story, the student is able to answer comprehension questions interjected by the teacher. | Answer factual questions about the story | Lesson 75 |
| Story questions—written<br>To teach the student to focus on the meaning of a story through written exercises | When given a question or an incomplete item on a story previously read, the student is able to do the exercise by remembering or rereading the story. | Circle *yes* or *no* in response to a written question | Take-Home 131 |
| | | Circle a word or words to complete a sentence | Take-Home 131 |
| | | Circle a word to replace a blank anywhere in a sentence. | Take-Home 144 |

**READ THE ITEMS**  **Range of Lessons: 151-160**

| Purpose of the track | Behavioral objectives | The student is asked to | First appears in |
|---|---|---|---|
| To teach the student to read and follow written instructions | When given written instructions, the student is able to read the instructions and perform the specified response to the teacher's action or words. | Read the item and respond with the specified action or words to the teacher's action or words | Lesson 151 |

| Purpose of the track | Behavioral objectives | The student is asked to | Tracing first appears in | Freehand first appears in |
|---|---|---|---|---|
| To teach the student how to print the symbols that represent sounds | *Tracing:* When given a printed symbol previously introduced in Sound Recognition, the student is able to trace the symbol. | Print the following symbols: | | |
| | | **a** | Take-Home 1 | Take-Home 21 |
| | | **m** | Take-Home 7 | Take-Home 23 |
| | | **s** | Take-Home 17 | Take-Home 22 |
| | *Writing freehand:* When given a printed symbol previously introduced and traced, the student is able to print the symbol freehand. | **ē** | Take-Home 19 | Take-Home 21 |
| | | **r** | Take-Home 24 | Take-Home 24 |
| | | **d** | Take-Home 28 | Take-Home 28 |
| | | **f** | Take-Home 32 | Take-Home 32 |
| | | **i** | Take-Home 35 | Take-Home 35 |
| | | **th** | Take-Home 39 | Take-Home 39 |
| | | **ī** | Take-Home 43 | Take-Home 43 |
| | | **n** | Take-Home 46 | Take-Home 46 |
| | | **c** | Take-Home 50 | Take-Home 50 |
| | | **o** | Take-Home 51 | Take-Home 51 |
| | | **ā** | Take-Home 61 | Take-Home 61 |
| | | **h** | Take-Home 63 | Take-Home 63 |
| | | **u** | Take-Home 66 | Take-Home 66 |
| | | **g** | Take-Home 70 | Take-Home 70 |
| | | **l** | Take-Home 73 | Take-Home 73 |
| | | **w** | Take-Home 78 | Take-Home 78 |
| | | **sh** | Take-Home 81 | Take-Home 81 |
| | | **Ī** | Take-Home 90 | Take-Home 90 |
| | | **k** | Take-Home 94 | Take-Home 94 |
| | | **ō** | Take-Home 99 | Take-Home 99 |
| | | **v** | Take-Home 103 | Take-Home 103 |
| | | **p** | Take-Home 109 | Take-Home 109 |
| | | **ch** | Take-Home 114 | Take-Home 117 |
| | | (continued) | | |

| Purpose of the track | Behavioral objectives | The student is asked to | Tracing first appears in | Freehand first appears in |
|---|---|---|---|---|
| | | Print the following symbols: | | |
| | | e | Take-Home 119 | Take-Home 119 |
| | | b | Take-Home 124 | Take-Home 124 |
| | | ɪ | Take-Home 128 | Take-Home 128 |
| | | y | Take-Home 133 | Take-Home 133 |
| | | x | Take-Home 141 | Take-Home 141 |
| | | J | Take-Home 146 | Take-Home 146 |
| | | ȳ | Take-Home 151 | Take-Home 151 |
| | | qu | Take-Home 155 | Take-Home 155 |
| | | z | Take-Home 157 | Take-Home 157 |
| | | ū | Take-Home 159 | Take-Home 159 |

## TAKE-HOME EXERCISES:  CROSS-OUT GAMES          Range of Lessons: 1-130

| Purpose of the track | Behavioral objectives | The student is asked to | First appears in |
|---|---|---|---|
| To teach the student visual discrimination of letters and words | When shown a specific sound symbol or word, the student is able to identify the same symbol or word wherever it appears in the exercise. | Cross out a specified sound symbol | Take-Home 1 |
| | | Cross out and circle specified sound symbols | Take-Home 42 |
| | | Cross out a specified word | Take-Home 86 |
| | | Cross out and circle specified words | Take-Home 124 |

## TAKE-HOME EXERCISES:  PICTURE COMPLETION          Range of Lessons: 1-39

| Purpose of the track | Behavioral objectives | The student is asked to | First appears in |
|---|---|---|---|
| To give the student practice in manipulating pencils and crayons | When given an unfinished picture, the student is able to trace the dotted line that completes the picture. | Follow a dotted line with a pencil or crayon to complete a picture | Take-Home 1 |

## TAKE-HOME EXERCISES:  SOUNDS/SOUND OUT          Range of Lessons: 14-33

| Purpose of the track | Behavioral objectives | The student is asked to | First appears in |
|---|---|---|---|
| To give the student practice in touching and saying sounds | When presented with one or two sounds written on an arrow, the student is able to touch and say the sound or sounds. | Touch and say one sound | Take-Home 14 |
| | | Touch under and say the sounds on an arrow slowly without stopping between sounds | Take-Home 19 |

| Purpose of the track | Behavioral objectives | The student is asked to | First appears in |
|---|---|---|---|
| To familiarize the student with the kinds of pattern recognition and comprehension activities often found in workbook activities and standardized tests | *Picture-sound patterns:* When given a pattern of a picture and a sound symbol, the student is able to recognize the pattern. | Reproduce a model pattern by filling in the missing sound symbol | Take-Home 21 |
| | *Two-sound patterns:* When given a pattern of two sound symbols, the student is able to recognize the pattern. | Reproduce a model pattern by filling in the missing sound symbol | Take-Home 40 |
| | | Recognize the model pattern in a row of patterns and cross out those patterns that differ from it | Take-Home 63 |
| | *Word-picture relationships:* When given a word and various pictures, the student is able to read the word and recognize which pictures correspond with it. | Identify which word and picture in a row correspond with each other and cross out the other word-picture combinations | Take-Home 70 |
| | | Identify and circle the picture that corresponds with a word | Take-Home 82 |
| | When given a picture and various words, the student is able to read the words and recognize which ones correspond with the picture. | Identify the word that corresponds with a picture and draw lines through the other words | Take-Home 114 |
| | | Draw a line connecting a word to a corresponding picture | Take-Home 126 |
| | *Sentence-picture relationships:* When given sentences and pictures, the student is able to read each sentence and recognize the corresponding picture. | Identify the sentence that corresponds with a picture and draw lines through the other sentences | Take-Home 120 |
| | | Draw a line connecting a sentence with the corresponding picture | Take-Home 131 |

| Purpose of the track | Behavioral objectives | The student is asked to | First appears in |
|---|---|---|---|
| To give the student additional practice in visual discrimination, pair relations, and word copying | When given a column of sounds or words in a column, the student is able to match each one to the same sound or word in another column. | Draw a line connecting two sound symbols that are the same | Take-Home 29 |
| | | Draw a line connecting two words that are the same | Take-Home 65 |
| | | Follow a line that connects a word with a blank and write the word in the blank | Take-Home 91 |

## TAKE-HOME EXERCISES: STORY AND SENTENCE COPYING

| Purpose of the track | Behavioral objectives | The student is asked to | First appears in |
|---|---|---|---|
| To teach the student to print words, phrases, and sentences | After tracing a dotted version of a word, phrase, or sentence from a story, the student is able to print it freehand. | Trace and print a word, phrase, or sentence | Take-Home 40 |

## TAKE-HOME EXERCISES: READING COMPREHENSION

| Purpose of the track | Behavioral objectives | The student is asked to | First appears in |
|---|---|---|---|
| To help the student extend skills learned in oral story-comprehension tasks, as well as those learned in sentence-saying and matching tasks | When given two complete sentences and the same two sentences with words missing, the student is able to complete the unfinished sentences. | Read an incomplete sentence and circle the word or words that complete it | Take-Home 120 |
| | When given a picture and two incomplete sentences that describe the picture, the student is able to complete the sentences. | Read an incomplete sentence and write the word that completes it | Take-Home 144 |

**Spelling Note:** Spelling lessons do not start with the first reading lesson. If the teacher is working with small groups, Spelling Lesson 1 is presented after a group completes Reading Lesson 50 in Presentation Book A. If the teacher is working with the entire class, Spelling Lesson 1 is presented after the lowest-performing group reaches Reading Lesson 40 in Presentation Book A.

## SPELLING BOOK: SOUND WRITING

**Range of Spelling Lessons: 1-108**

| Purpose of the track | Behavioral objectives | The student is asked to | First appears in |
|---|---|---|---|
| To give the student practice in writing sounds | When the teacher says one or more sounds, the student is able to repeat and write the sound or sounds. | Repeat and write the following sounds: | |
| | | i | Spelling Lesson 1 |
| | | r | Spelling Lesson 1 |
| | | a | Spelling Lesson 3 |
| | | t | Spelling Lesson 7 |
| | | n | Spelling Lesson 10 |
| | | f | Spelling Lesson 13 |
| | | o | Spelling Lesson 16 |
| | | m | Spelling Lesson 20 |
| | | s | Spelling Lesson 31 |
| | | h | Spelling Lesson 34 |
| | | u | Spelling Lesson 43 |
| | | d | Spelling Lesson 54 |
| | | e | Spelling Lesson 61 |
| | | w | Spelling Lesson 64 |
| | | l | Spelling Lesson 68 |
| | | c | Spelling Lesson 83 |
| | | b | Spelling Lesson 95 |
| | | th | Spelling Lesson 102 |
| | | p | Spelling Lesson 107 |

**SPELLING BOOK: SAY THE SOUNDS**

**Range of Spelling Lessons: 5-11**

| Purpose of the track | Behavioral objectives | The student is asked to | First appears in |
|---|---|---|---|
| To teach the student that words are composed of distinct sounds | When the teacher says a word at a normal rate, the student is able to say the word slowly—one sound at a time—without pausing between sounds. | Say the sounds in words with two sounds | Spelling Lesson 5 |


**SPELLING BOOK: WORD WRITING**

**Range of Spelling Lessons: 9-111**

| Purpose of the track | Behavioral objectives | The student is asked to | First appears in |
|---|---|---|---|
| To give the student practice in hearing and writing sounds in words | When the teacher says a word, the student is able to spell the word by saying the sounds in the word and then writing the word. | Say the sounds in a word, pausing between each sound<br><br>Write the sounds in a word; then read the word | Spelling Lesson 9<br><br>Spelling Lesson 9 |


**SPELLING BOOK: SENTENCE WRITING**

**Range of Spelling Lessons: 82-111**

| Purpose of the track | Behavioral objectives | The student is asked to | First appears in |
|---|---|---|---|
| To give the student practice in spelling and writing the words in a sentence | When the teacher says a sentence, the student is able to repeat the sentence slowly and then write the sentence with each word spelled correctly and with a period at the end. | Say a sentence, pausing between each word; then write the sentence | Spelling Lesson 82 |

**NOTES:**